SCIEI
THE WILD

Adventures
of a Zoologist

U. H. Kullnick

EDITION EXOVO
Copyright © 2013 Uwe Kullnick
Set in 12pt Verdana
Dr. Uwe Kullnick
Translated by Melvyn Morgan
uwe.kullnick@email.de
Munich, Germany
Cover design Uwe Kullnick, Photo © Werner Dreblow
ISBN: 1494751062
ISBN-13 978-1494751067

CONTENTS

ACKNOWLEDGMENTS

Thanks to the animals which have not eaten, poisoned, squashed, strangled, drowned or bit me. But without these near incidents my life would be poor and meaningless.

THE PORCUPINE POLKA

Africa! What comes to mind when I ask you about Africa? Perhaps you think of lions, elephants, the heat, the jungle and of adventures? Boys probably remember that the football World Cup was in South Africa. But it's the animals which are really the most important thing, especially since you know some of them from zoos or from the TV. Surely you can also remember hippos and rhinoceroses and, oh yes, giraffes, those giants with long necks, and the softest eyes and longest eyelashes that you've ever seen.

But it's no doubt the girls who love the giraffes, the boys have probably never noticed their long eyelashes at all, have you?

Boys are probably more interested in dangerous animals. In their imagination lions and leopards roam the savannah looking for prey, but hyenas too aren't to be scoffed at. Giant crocodiles are just as great as snakes, leopards and tigers, – but hang on a moment something is not quite right here. Ah, I know! Tigers! – Tigers live in India and Siberia but not in Africa. Well, you know, sometimes it's really not easy to remember where all the animals come from. But I think that as long as no-one comes up with the idea of putting kangaroos into the African jungle, then it's not so bad.

When they think of Africa many people think of wild animals. I, too, was no different when I was a child. By the time I'd finished school I'd learnt many things about all kinds of animals in the world. But the ones in Africa were my favourites. I was very lucky that my uncle had a kiosk in Frankfurt Zoo. What do you mean by lucky? Well it's obvious - I was allowed to spend the summer holidays in this zoo.

For six weeks I spent every day with the animals. I was eight years old and was in the second year at school, so I was still a little boy. The keepers took to me at once and showed me everything. I was even there when an okapi was born for the first time in a zoo. Okapis are very, very rare animals that live deep in the African jungle. They look like a hybrid between a zebra and a giraffe and I think that they are really beautiful. But birth in a zoo is another story.

As you can imagine, I learnt a lot of things in the zoo about animal behaviour . To this very day I've not forgotten much and it's helped me many times to find the right way to treat wild animals.

A few years ago, when I had grown-up, I was given the opportunity to take part in research in Tanzania. Tanzania is a big country in Africa, near the equator. The animals I mentioned before live here, except the tiger of course, but you know that . Ah yes, I wanted to tell you about the research work. It was about...

No, no, it would be much too boring if I told you about it straight away. Perhaps you can guess the animal that we actually wanted to study?

It's as big as a large dog but really slim. It has yellow fur with black spots and a very long tail with a white tuft at the end. So, have you got an idea already?

It's a predator and has very long legs which it needs for running. It's the fastest land-living creature on earth. Yes of course, it's a cheetah. When they're hunting, they run as quickly as a car can drive on the road.

That's all very interesting, I can hear you say, but what's all that got to do with a porcupine? A great deal, as you will see!In Tanzania cheetahs often live where there are cattle ranches. Many farmers think that the wild cats eat the young calves of their cows. For this reason they often drive away the cheetahs and even shoot them dead, although it's forbidden. Some biologists, who came from Frankfurt Zoo to Tanzania, wanted to find out if the cheetahs were really a danger to the young calves. I took part in this research for a few weeks and helped in the observation of the animals. My plane flew directly from Germany to the Kilimanjaro airstrip in the middle of Africa. Kilimanjaro is a very high mountain on which there's always snow, even in summer. I was very excited and did not know what to expect. A nice young coloured man was waiting for me with a cardboard sign with my name on it. The man who picked me up at the airfield was an African gamekeeper. He'd been waiting for me, together with Lisa, until my plane had landed.

Lisa had come with another plane shortly before me and he'd picked her up just like he had me. We drove for many hours to the camp. On the way we told him that we were very much looking forward to Africa and the cheetahs, to which he smiled broadly. We were both very excited. Everything was strange for us. Everything here looked very different to things we knew at home. The thing we noticed the most was the many people who were walking at the side of the road. They wandered along the dusty road, either alone or in small groups.

Most of them were Maasai warriors. Perhaps you know that they are nomads who, in the past, hunted lions armed only with spears. They are a very brave and proud people.

Later I met many of them. All of them were very friendly and helpful. The greatest thing about them was their shoes. Very often, they were bits of rubber, cut from old car tyres, which were exactly as long as their feet. Leather laces were thread through the rubber at the sides. They were fixed to their feet. This made them into a sort of sandal, like we wear in summer. That is just the thing for this dusty, stony region full of prickly bushes. No thorns would go through those tyre shoes.

The scientists in the camp gave us a very friendly welcome. They immediately invited us to have a barbecue with them around the camp fire. Shortly after this we went to bed. Although it was still early in the evening. At first I was puzzled, but Richard explained that we had to get up very early to find the animals. "And then you often have to travel a long way until you see any at all. You mustn't believe that here in Africa you could just come across warthogs, antelopes, zebras, elephants or even the very rare cheetahs just by chance. Not one bit. The animals are usually a long way away and often turn up where you least expect them ", he said. And that's just what happened in my first night in Africa.

I was in a tent together with Richard. After the long journey I fell asleep immediately. I had no idea what was about to happen during the night. Suddenly a noise woke me You've probably seen what happens when a dog is sleeping in the living room or in the garden. Suddenly he pricks up his ears and stares in the direction that the noise has come from. He doesn't move an inch while he is doing this. Imagine that was exactly what was happening to me too. Only, of course I can't prick up my ears as well as a sheepdog. But, apart from that everything was the same. I felt like my camp bed was in a dark cave, deep under the earth, that's how dark it was. The noise that had woken me sounded like the thunder of a faraway storm. But somehow or other it sounded a little different to thunder.

"Just stay as you are and don't move", Richard whispered . "If you don't scare or anger them, they won't bother you. Every now and then they come into the camp. They're only curious."

Then I heard the noise again. It really was just like thunder. Only it sounded as if it was directly in front of the tent. But it was much, much quieter than thunder. Now I could feel that something was feeling its way along the side of the tent. As it was doing this it came up against my camp bed, and as a result I almost fell out of it. And then it was all over. Anxiously I whispered to Richard: "Are those lions by any chance?" No reply. Perhaps he had already fallen asleep again?

He whispered back, "No, don't worry. It's only elephants. A whole family. We know them well and they know us, too."

I opened my eyes even wider, but of course I couldn't see a thing in the dark.

"Don't they knock over the tents?"

"No, there's no need to be afraid of them. They stay here for a little while and then they disappear again." I continued to listen out and was still trembling under my blanket.

"They smell you and that is why they come. They want to see if you or Lisa are dangerous for them and their young. Your smell is new and that's the reason that they came into the camp. So really only because of you and Lisa."

"Phew, us a danger to the elephants? Who'd have thought it?", I said.

"By the way, the light thunder sound that you heard comes from the elephants' stomachs. They eat enormous amounts of grass and leaves and that gives them severe wind." At that moment, a thundery sound came once more from behind the tent.

"Do you see what I mean?"

I had to smile and then I was no longer so afraid. How can you be afraid of farting elephants?

The invisible creatures on the other side of the thin canvas stayed for a while in the camp. Later on I heard them leaving softly and finally it became quiet once more. I was no longer afraid and I'd almost fallen asleep once more. Richard was also softly snoring again. "Awoooo" came a howling sound from very close by. It sounded really scary. But I already knew what the sound was and it did not scare me. It was a jackal. It was probably looking for something to eat in the camp and was only howling out of disappointment, because we'd cleaned everything away.

I was looking forward to the next day and then fell asleep. It was still dark when Richard, John, Lisa and I set off in our research car, a Range Rover with four-wheel-drive. Just where were we going to? To the cheetahs, of course. To be exact, we were travelling to the traps designed to catch the animals.

Why did they need to be caught? Well, a lot of animals move around the whole day long. They're looking for food and the cheetahs follow in order to prey on them. We had to observe them for our research . We wanted to catch them to place a sort of dog collar on them. These special kind of collars have a radio transmitter.

With the use of the roof antenna on our Range Rover or a portable antenna and a computer we could see exactly where they were wandering around in this huge area. Then we would drive there, observe what they did and exactly what they hunted and ate. The biologists guessed that the cheetahs mostly hunted rabbits, wild boar, small antelopes or scrub hares. But they had never seen that they had caught calves. If they showed evidence of this, the farmers would no longer need to worry about their young calves. Then they would probably leave the cheetahs in peace. But the scientists had not reached this stage. They still had to make a number of observations to convince the farmers and this is where Lisa and I could help.

To give a cheetah a collar you could always pin a note to a tree on which it says: Everyone come here and pick up a collar. "You can take a running jump!" is what the dear creatures would say. So, there is no alternative but to catch them alive in traps.

Live traps are really big cages which they can fit in without injuring themselves. Imagine a cage which is bigger than a large dog-kennel.

There are iron bars everywhere and gates at the front and back which can be pulled up. You put this box in a place where you think that the cheetahs will pass by, for instance by one of their scratching posts. You hang a big piece of meat inside it and leave the front cage door open. So when a hungry cheetah passes by he creeps carefully towards the trap. He gently takes one step at a time, creeps inside the box and at some stage comes directly next to the bait with his nose. Hmmmmm, how tasty that smells. When he bites into the bait, he steps on a rocker on the floor. As a result, the raised cage door drops down as quick as lightning and the animal is caught in the trap. Uninjured, but of course really terrified, he tries to get out, but he cannot. It is impossible. In such a moment cheetahs do exactly what we would do.

They moan and groan a bit. But at some time or other they eat a little of the bait and wait and see what will happen to them.

On this morning we hoped, of course, that there would be a cheetah in one of our traps. Lisa and I were looking forward to this terrifically. We would sedate him with a dart from a blowpipe and place the collar on him. While he was sleeping we could examine him to make sure that he was healthy. We also wanted to know, of course, if it was a male or female. And in the end the cheetah would be set free again.

That was our plan. But as very often in life, plans don't always work out. You imagine something to be so good, and when it comes about, things go wrong. That's the way things are sometimes. And that's exactly what happened to us when we came to our first trap. We could see from a distance that something was moving in it. As a bush was blocking half the view, we could not recognise if it was a cheetah. Richard moved carefully towards it to see what was caught in the trap.

He waved and laughed and we came a little nearer. Our jaws dropped with disappointment. It was not even a cheetah or any other kind of predator. No, it was a porcupine. A big, fully grown and very offended porcupine was sat in a corner of the trap and was looking sadly out of the cage.

Finally! One or two of you probably thought that there'd be no porcupine at all in this story. No such luck. Now this is where the story of the porcupine polka really starts. Richard said that we should practise how to deal with wild animals which got caught in these traps.

"You can't simply go up to it and lift up the cage door, even if it's not a predator in this case. It's a wild animal, it has dangerous quills and it is very afraid of us. If you're not careful, you can quickly end up with a lot of quills in your legs or wherever. Even big lions have a great deal of respect for porcupines and normally leave them in peace. So, always be really careful."

We nodded. Lisa and I were the new ones and one of us now had to release the porcupine. Now, boys often have a big mouth when it comes down to talking about dangerous things. But when it gets really serious it is often the girls who go forward bravely and deliberately. This was the case here, too. But before things really get going, it is time to introduce both of them to you. Lisa and the porcupine or perhaps better the other way around, first the porcupine and then his rescuer, Lisa.

The name PORC-upine alone is actually wrong. Because it's really a rodent. They are related to hares, beavers and hamsters. However, they're much bigger. The animals can defend themselves extremely well. They live on the ground, dig deep tunnels and openings and are naturally , like all rodents, vegetarians. With their long quills they're as tall as a big Golden Retriever. They have a blunt black snout and their quills are very long in some places. Particularly on their bottoms there are some which are as long as an arrow. The quills are black and white and have nasty little barbs on their pointed ends. But the most dangerous thing about these quills is that they're loose. When they have hit an animal, they often break off. Then they stick in the skin or the fur and are terribly painful. So, although porcupines are really quite nice little animals, it's better not to get too near to them. And now Lisa was supposed to release such a dangerous animal from the cage. This was sure to be exciting.

OK. But now over to Lisa. She was not very tall, not that strong and she had no idea how you dealt with porcupines. Just like me, she didn't know how you release a wild animal from a trap. Lisa was wearing leather shorts, light brown desert boots and thick socks which poked out of the shoes.

When Richard asked which of us wanted to release the animal, Lisa bravely took one step forward. I looked at her questioningly as she went off with Richard. But she put on a brave face. They went close up to the cage. They whispered so that they would not scare the porcupine. John and I remained some distance away.

The porcupine grunted. It sounded just like a little piglet. And just as sweetly it pressed its blunt little black snout between the bars of the cage door. Its black eyes sparkled and sometimes it hopped with all four of its legs in the air at the same time. It really looked very cute. If only it hadn't rattled its quills in such a threatening manner at the same time.

When Lisa came up to the cage, the animal had a huge fright. It turned around and sped to the other end of the cage. At the same time it now squealed almost like a real pig and rattled its quills threateningly once more.

These quills are as hard as those of a hedgehog, only much longer, and they are not so closely spaced. Most of them are located on the bottom and short tail of the animal. So if it wants to defend itself, it turns its bottom towards its attacker. And that is exactly what it now did. Lisa was clearly the enemy. Never mind the shorts and the nice smile, there was something strange going on here.

Lisa quickly climbed onto the cage and held on to the branch of a tree. She talked to the porcupine like you would talk to a dog. She called it Willy. Willy was now making a terrible noise in the cage. He ran from one end to the other and kept looking up at Lisa.

"Steady, Willy, steady, I'm not going to do anything to you", she said, but what she probably meant was: "Please be good and don't do anything to me." But it was not so important, because I think that both were afraid. Willy was afraid of the big human above his head and Lisa was afraid of those long rattling quills. Now Lisa wanted to open the rear cage door so that Willy could disappear. The plan was that he would run into the bush opposite us and go into hiding once more. That was exactly what she wanted, but what did he do?

He remained cowering in his corner; and although Lisa had pulled up and fixed the cage door, Willy didn't want to go away. He stood there and looked out of the cage. He sniffed and surveyed the scene, but he stayed cowering in the trap. Lisa got braver and braver. She hopped about on top of the cage to drive Willy out. Willy grunted, looked up and jumped about, too.

Lisa coaxed him like you coax chickens. "Pah, pah, pah, Willy, come, clear off." This seemed to please Willy and the rattling of his quills became quieter. Nevertheless, he remained in the trap.

Lisa now went to the other end of the cage. Willy came with her. She went back again. Willy followed her on the ground. Meanwhile, his grunting had turned to a whistle. It now almost seemed as if the porcupine wanted to lure Lisa into the cage. Not a great prospect for Lisa.

"Lift up the front cage door, too", shouted Richard. So that we would not get in Willy's path we three went to the car. Lisa bent down, grabbed the front cage door and pulled it up. "Go, Willy, go away, clear off", called Lisa and we hoped that it would work now. Willy looked blankly around and then back up to Lisa's boots. There was something incredibly fascinating that he found about her. He simply didn't want to go away. Lisa ran up and down on top of the cage. Not a hope. Willy remained adamantly sitting in the trap or just ran backwards and forwards. Actually, we could've gone off at this point. At some time or other Willy would've cleared off. However, Lisa was still on top of the trap and could not climb down. Both cage doors were open and Willy was lurking in the cage below her. Lisa could not simply climb down, as that was too dangerous due to Willy's quills.

Just why did he not want to leave the cage? Lisa began to whistle, Willy whistled too, Lisa cursed, Willy grunted. Lisa spoke to us. Willy squeaked. What could be done?

Now, you have to know that porcupines are brave creatures who are able to defend themselves and that even leopards and elephants have respect for them and their sharp quills. However, they have a big disadvantage, they are stupid. No, you can say that they are very stupid and stubborn and obstinate. I don't like saying it, but sometimes they can be simply plain dumb. So, somehow or other we had to trick Willy. Before we had set off in the morning, Lisa and I had been given whistles. Richard had explained to us that "It may happen that one of you gets lost in the bush and cannot see the others any more. If this happens we blow the whistles hard. And this is how we find each other again."

We shouted to Lisa that she should use her whistle and jump up and down on the cage at the same time. Lisa grinned, then she blew on her whistle and danced around on the cage like a chimpanzee gone mad. Stupid Willy seemed to find this simply cool and he sat in the middle of the cage and watched Lisa dancing. Richard then had a super idea. We got into the car and drove carefully up to the cage. The car's bonnet was pointing at the front cage door.

Now we were so near to the cage that Lisa could climb onto the car without Willy being able to catch her. While we were watching Lisa moving carefully onto the car, nobody paid any attention to Willy. When we looked again he had gone. Where had he gone to? He had not run off, because then we would have seen him on the other side of the cage. He couldn't possibly be lurking under the car, could he? What could we do now? Nobody wanted to get out, as they would probably get a dose of porcupine quills on their feet or on their legs. Drive off? No, then we would probably have run Willy over. You'll remember, porcupines are really dumb.

Therefore, we believed that Willy would now find it really super to wait under the car.

We looked at each other helplessly. Until I had a dazzling idea. I bent forward to the steering wheel from my seat at the back and sounded the horn like mad. All of a sudden, Willy shot out of his hiding place. He ran back into the cage as if he was being chased by all the lions in Africa. As he was doing this he stumbled over his short legs, did a somersault and lost a few quills. Then he got back on his feet and ran back under the car.

But now it seemed as though Willy had had enough of the game. He ran as quickly as a porcupine can under our car and came out at the back near the exhaust . Now there was no stopping him and he ran and ran and ran. We watched him until he was nothing more than a dust cloud. Then he completely disappeared .

Richard said that he'd released many porcupines from traps, but he'd never seen one like Willy before. "It must have been because of the way that Lisa got him to dance", he said with a laugh. John had taken photos the whole time and showed us them on his camera. He called it the porcupine polka, and we laughed ourselves silly. For the whole of the time that we were in Africa, Lisa had to listen to the story of the porcupine polka. And every time that we saw one in the scrub, we wondered if it was possibly Willy.

The time in Tanzania went by much too quickly, but we still managed to catch many cheetahs and to place radio collars on them.

Together with the biologists we were also able to observe that the cheetahs only very rarely hunted young calves. Since then the farmers have tolerated having the cheetahs near to their cattle and no longer shoot them.

On the flight home I took a last look at the snow-covered Kilimanjaro. Then we flew into the night. As I was going to sleep my thoughts went back to the first day in the bush, and I had to have a little laugh to myself at the super porcupine polka.

Yes, of course I collected the porcupine quills that Willy had lost in the trap. I took them home with me, and if you come and visit me, you can take a look at them, too.

AN OCTOPUS RUNS AWAY

So, what do you know about octopuses? No, I don't mean the giant octopuses in fairy-tales and ancient stories where sea monsters attack ships and pull them under water. That's all nonsense if you ask me, but those kind of stories are so wonderfully creepy.

Now and again you can find octopuses, yes that really is the plural form, in a fishmonger's and in some restaurants they often end up on your plate as baby octopus. If truth be told, octopus does not even taste very good. It's often eaten with garlic sauce, because otherwise it would taste of nothing at all.

But that's not what I want to tell you about today. I am talking about those interesting fellows who live in the sea and which look a bit like a squashed balloon with eight tubes coming out of it. These are the sea creatures which you sometimes see on the television and often in aquariums at zoos. I am a zoologist and therefore I am particularly interested in their behaviour, their life in the sea and so on.

So, what do you know about octopuses? Probably not very much. But you've really missed out on something there. They're wonderful creatures. The first wonderful thing is that they have eight legs which go from their head and which are called tentacles. Their true scientific name is cephalopod but their common name is octopus. That comes from the Greek word "octo" which means eight, because of their eight arms, and "pod" for foot. So, octopus means eight-footed one. That is really simple and easy to remember.

And it's really crazy what they can do with their tentacles. I myself experienced how Paulino, an octopus, led my colleagues and I in Naples, that's in Italy, a merry dance again and again.

A while ago I was doing some research at the zoological station in Naples. But in English that does not sound special at all. For the real effect, you have to hear it in Italian - Stazione Zoologica di Napoli, now that sounds a lot better doesn't it? Napoli, that is to say Naples, is on the Mediterranean coast, very near to a volcano. Its name is Vesuvius. The Italians call it Vesuvio. Somehow or other, I think that is sounds much more musical in Italian, don't you think?

There's a huge public aquarium at this maritime station which is open to visitors. Every day school classes from Naples, as well as visitors from the surrounding region, would come to admire the many sea creatures. Of course, they saw the front part of the many aquariums and the fish, crabs and turtles inside. But there was also a hidden, secret part. That was the section of the public pools from which the creatures were fed which began at the back of the pools and then led into the deepest parts of the cellar of the incredibly old building. This is where the story begins of Paulino, Professore Lupo, his daughter, Angelina, the fishermen, Pietro and Tomaso and of course myself. I think that it is interesting enough to tell you about it.

On the first morning after I had arrived I wanted to go down into the dark cellar rooms of the aquarium before breakfast. You could hear the slightly muffled sound of the city traffic in Naples in the public area of the aquarium. Engines screamed, tires screeched and trucks rumbled along the narrow streets. You could also hear the sound of pedestrians, cyclists and moped riders. Everyone complained about the chaotic traffic in Naples. But the thing you noticed most about Naples was that people sounded their horn all the time. Everyone in Naples who has a horn honks it constantly. You can't get anywhere without sounding your horn. And anyone who doesn't have a horn is on the receiving end of the honking and in this way is shooed from the road or from a zebra-crossing. It's very different to life on our roads.

For every stone step that I descended from the entrance hall, the noise disappeared bit by bit. From step to step it became quieter and quieter until deep down in the third level of the cellar rooms it was completely silent. Well, you could not say that there were no sounds at all, because everywhere there was the uncanny sound of bubbling, gurgling and swishing. All the fish pools were supplied from here with sea-water from the Gulf of Naples. Here were the aquariums with the fish which first had to get used to the conditions inside the station before they could join the other creatures above in the public aquariums. The laboratory animals had their pools here in this cellar.

But one thing at a time. As I very carefully stepped on the last, damp and somewhat slippery step and turned around the corner in the dim light, a huge mouth appeared in front of me and snapped at me. I jumped back with a start and nearly fell on my backside.

But there was no danger at all. The moray eel, which lived in its burrow here in a pool, was just as shocked as I was and only wanted to ward me off by opening its mouth. Phew, I can tell you, I was really nervous after this welcome and my heart was beating like mad. After we had both recognised that we were no danger to each other I went on a little more assured. From the next aquarium a huge sea turtle stared at me through the glass pane of its living room. Its thick snout looked capable of breaking the glass in one go. We looked deeply into each other's eyes and then it slowly turned its bottom towards me and swam off.

I passed by sea-horses and starfish and then ... I saw Nemo. Of course, it was not really Nemo from the film who was just trying to hide in a sea-anemone, he is just a cartoon character. Instead it was one of the anemone fish who look just like Nemo. In the film they are really cute, but in real life they are much, much prettier. They wind around close to the poisonous tentacles of the sea-anemones. That protects them against predatory fish which want to snap them up. The anemone fish are not bothered by the poison of the sea-anemones. They are really very special fish. All anemone fish are born as males. In a shoal there is only a single female. If she dies or is eaten by predator fish, the strongest male becomes a female and can also lay eggs.

Whatever, what I really wanted to do was to move on to Paulino.

Then I came to the biggest pool. Here I had a really eerie sensation. Imagine a huge, round pool made of glass. In this pool three big sharks were waiting to be transferred to a much bigger pool in the public area of the station where other sharks were already living.

The three sharks swam around in the clear water in an eerily calm manner. Each one of them was at least two metres long. They swam quite calmly through the pool and when they came to the front part their eyes followed my movements exactly. It seemed to me that they were opening up their huge mouths with the rows of huge, super-sharp teeth even wider especially for me and were just grinning at me. But today I am sure that I was of no interest to them. That is just the way that sharks look.

A little further on, in a corner of the dark room, was Paulino's pool. I had met the octopus briefly on the previous evening. Today I had to look very carefully. One side of his body looked just like the thick brown stone which had been placed in the pool for decoration. However, his tentacles had exactly the same colour as the air stone which was blowing the air bubbles into the pool. It was amazing how well he could camouflage himself.

"He's bored", was what Tomaso had said. Tomaso was one of the fishermen who caught the sea creatures from the Gulf of Naples for the researchers at the Stazione. He went to the next pool, fed the sea bass and we both went up the stairs together. That was on the first evening.

But now I have to introduce you to Paulino . What did he look like? Hmmm. It was a bit strange, but he looked like a wobbly lump of jelly with legs. But first of all his skin colour. It was, how should I say, ... changeable is probably the right word. I will explain it to you a bit later on if that is OK.

His very supple legs, the tentacles, looked just like thick snakes. He was continuously fidgeting around with them, back and forth, just like a bored schoolboy. On each of Paulino's tentacles, you will remember there are eight of them, are lots of discs made of skin. These discs are called suckers. An octopus has at least a hundred of these suckers. Paulino could hold onto everything with them, with a strength you just won't believe for a creature which looks so wobbly.

Such an octopus can climb up panes of glass and even unscrew jam jar lids. It is said that octopuses are just as clever as parrots. And an octopus has big eyes. He looks at you with these as to say "I'm bored to death, will you play with me?"

On this morning I wanted to fetch him to see how he goes about camouflaging himself to look like a stone, a plant, the sea-bed or even like a chess board.

I thought that his camouflage on that day was particularly good. I could not see him at all. When I looked more closely I could see that he was not in his burrow and also not behind the rock. He had not disguised himself as if he was a section of the gravel in the aquarium, and octopuses are definitely not capable of making themselves transparent or invisible. Then it gradually dawned on me "He's cleared off." I checked the pool in disbelief. Everything seemed to be sealed correctly. At the back, near the water inlet, was a tiny gap, but this was much too small for Paulino, he could not have got out there. Or that is what I thought. But he had disappeared nonetheless. So there I stood, early in the morning, alone in this cold cellar, in the dim light, being watched suspiciously by three sharks, staring into an empty aquarium.

"Has he disappeared again?", asked a deep voice behind me.

I jumped with a start. I saw Professore Lupo with his mouth open and a questioning look on his face.

"He often clears off. He can get through everywhere where he can fit his snout", he said. By the way, octopuses do not have a proper mouth but rather a hard snout which looks a bit like that of a parrot. I looked at Professore Lupo incredulously . Then he explained to me: "I really do think that he has pressed open this tiny crack at the water inlet and has got out through it."

"Through that tiny hole? It's much too small."

"You have no idea. We have to hurry. He can stand being out of water for a long time, but he will suffocate if he is exposed to the air for too long, just like fish on dry land."

"I know, I hope we find him soon", I replied.

Professore Lupo called Tomaso, Pietro and his daughter, Angelina, and we started to hunt.

"Look at first near to the pool, in dark corners. Watch out, because he bites if you touch him and he can wind his arms really tightly around your hands using his suckers. You can hardly get rid of him."

I had a funny feeling, because I had never touched a living octopus. I had absolutely no experience with squid which is another name for the octopus. When you make them angry, they squirt a kind of ink. In the sea the predator fish believes that he has landed in a big dark cloud and in the meantime the octopus simply disappears through the back door.

Professore Lupo shouted, "I'll just go to the toilet first, carry on searching." I thought to myself that he had all the time in the world. He is sending us out to look and he is sneaking off. Angelina saw my doubtful look.

"No. no, it's not what you think. Last time Paulino was in the loo and was hiding in the bowl. At least there was water there and he could breathe. Octopuses are incredibly smart. Paulino had got lost and sensed the water. He had lifted up the toilet seat and crept inside. We were glad that he didn't clear off down the waste pipe", she said laughing. Paulino rescued himself into toilet

I did not show whether I believed her or not and instead began searching.

Tomaso said, "You must look in all the pools. He gets in somewhere and looks for something to eat or when he's been in the air too long"

"Until he himself is eaten one day", grunted Pietro and took a disapproving look into towards the shark pool. I quickly went to the huge moray eel who you probably remember from before. But I neither saw Paulino there, nor remains of him. I gave a sigh of relief.

Professore Lupo returned and called to us that Paulino was not hiding in the toilet this time and that he himself would go to the electric eels and that we should on all accounts take a look inside every empty water container which stood around in the cellar as an overflow for new fish arriving. Nothing, Paulino had simply disappeared. Then Pietro came up with the idea of taking a look in the scullery. The researchers' laboratory apparatus and aquarium equipment was cleaned there.

While I was on my stomach on the floor and looking under the cupboards, Angelina was hidden between the water barrels and Tomaso was taking a close look once again at the sharks pool. Then Pietro returned whistling happily. He was carrying a container, not much bigger than a flat waste bin and he called, "Here he is, the rogue." With one hand he carried the plastic bowl and with the other he was pressing down a lid on it with all his might. Nevertheless, two tentacles snaked their way out and felt around him. One arm probed into his nostril. The other attached a sucker to the lens of his glasses and pulled them off his nose.

"Quick, help me, I must bring him back into his pool", he shouted, laughing at the same time.

Finally we were all standing in front of the pool. I replaced the covering plate and quickly blocked off his escape hole. We watched Paulino, looking perfectly cute, as he set about the prawns that Tomaso had thrown into the pool as fodder.

That was my first experience of a break-out by Paulino. In the following days and weeks I carried out many successful behavioural experiments on him and we built up a friendship. And I am also certain that he recognised me after a few days. He knew exactly that I would bring him a prawn in the morning and during our work together he received a little piece of fish to eat, which seemed to please him a lot.

But now I must keep my promise and say something about the colour of octopuses, because that also had a lot to do with my experiments. Octopuses are world champions in camouflaging. In their skin they have a lot of really tiny coloured bags which are only visible as microscopic-sized dots. But when they want to, they can increase the size of these bags and take on virtually any pattern and many colours. They can do this so well that you can hardly tell the difference between them and the sea-bed or the decorations in the aquarium.

There have been experiments in which a marble chess-board has been placed into the pool. The animals really attempt to imitate this pattern on the surface of their bodies. They've only failed to imitate the corners of the black and white squares of the chess-board. But at first sight their skin looked like a chess-board. But they can also turn purple with rage when sly scientists place experimental equipment in their pool and the octopuses have to think about what they could be. This camouflage is a wonderful skill. No creature on the earth can do this, perhaps with the exception of a chameleon, but I can tell you about that another time. In any case, I learned a lot about Paulino during those weeks.

But one day everything changed. I had returned Paulino to his pool in the afternoon and had given him a lumpfish as a reward. Lumpfish are giant slug-like creatures who live in the sea. They weigh almost half a pound, a good weight and a really good dinner for Paulino.

For some reason or other I was not at ease. Before I went to my hotel I went down into the cellar to see how Paulino had got on with the lumpfish. All you could see in the water was a huge reddish-bluish cloud. Now, octopuses can squirt out such clouds of ink and I knew that lumpfish could do the same, and so I thought that they'd just squirted ink at each other. So I waited until the water had been cleared by the pumps. But what did I see? Just the lumpfish. Totally unharmed, the sea slug was happily chewing away at the entrance to Paulino's burrow. And Paulino? He was gone.

We searched everywhere again for him. Toilet, water overflow containers, all the other pools, the scullery and everywhere you can think of. But Paulino was nowhere to be found. What had happened? I'd forgotten to place one of the heavy sandbags on the covering plate. Therefore it would have been easy for him to lift one up. He would've had no problem at all without the weight of the sandbag to hold it down. I'd seen him doing this. He tested out the edge of the pool, inch by inch, until he found a crack somewhere or other in which the tip of one of his tentacles would fit. But he found no gap. Paulino stuck his suckers onto the surface of the glass underneath the cover and pressed his body with all of his might upwards until the cover moved. Then he pushed one of his eight tentacles into the gap that he had created and took a break. He forced a second arm through and pressed with all the strength he had from below. A real gap had hardly appeared before he had pushed his second tentacle through.

Now four of his arms were outside the pool, but his big body and the remaining four arms were still inside. He made himself really flat. Now Paulino looked like a pizza with eight legs which was trying to creep through a closed door. Hey presto! And the centre part of his body had slipped through and he wanted to clear off. That time I caught him and crammed him back into the pool. I placed the cover on the pool and then the sandbag on top of that and just said to him "Gotcha, Paulino! People are really smarter than you!" That was a few days before, and since that time he had remained well-behaved in his pool.

But now he had really disappeared. We looked for hours, into the late evening. I even spent the night down there so that I could help him if he appeared anywhere and tried to get into a pool.

When Professore Lupo went home he said to me "If Paulino hasn't found a way into the water, he'll be dead by now. No octopus can survive for so long out of water. He's most certainly suffocated." You can't imagine how sad I was and because he didn't appear in the following days my mood didn't get any better.

My experiments had to wait, because Pietro and Tomaso were unable to catch another suitable octopus, and so I took a trip to Vesuvius. That's the volcano which I spoke about earlier on. 2000 years ago there was a terrible eruption and a whole town was buried under its ash and lava. Today you can visit the town, the remains of which have been excavated. It was very strange to walk along the empty streets and to imagine what it must have been like when it rained ash.

When I returned from my trip everybody was extremely agitated.

"Paulino is back", Angelina shouted to me from a distance away. Delighted, I ran up to her.

"Can you imagine it? He was in the shark pool the whole of the time", she said

"In the shark pool? And the sharks didn't eat him ?"

"He's found a good hiding place where they can't get at him", said Angelina, grinning from ear to ear.

"Papa says we can't get him out of there. The sharks are too dangerous."

The situation was hopeless. What could we do? Someone could climb in and catch him. Bu could you endanger the life of a human for an octopus? That was impossible. Could you leave him there? Somehow or other that too was not right. Then I had an idea.

Paulino had probably not dared to leave his hiding-place and therefore he had not eaten for a few days. I immediately fetched a crab from the food container and tied a string around its shell. I lowered it gently into the pool, directly in front of the octopus's hiding-place. In this way I thought that I could probably lure him out and catch him with the net. I knew that he'd not be able to resist a crab. Tomaso und Pietro positioned themselves on either side of me, each with a long wooden pole in their hands. If it was necessary they wanted to keep the sharks away from Paulino with them. Angelina held onto me so that I could lean forward without falling in the water. Professore Lupo went to the other side of the circular pool and observed all the activities from there. The crab waved its legs about wildly while I was lowering it to Paulino. I think that it wasn't too happy at the prospect of entering a pool with three sharks where a hungry octopus was also waiting . The Professore suddenly raised his hand. LOOK OUT! Paulino had seemingly spotted the crab and had slid a tentacle out of his hiding-place. But he wasn't the only one who'd developed an interest. Both of the blue sharks were looking around interestedly at the new creature in the pool and came carefully nearer. But they were scared off by Tomaso's and Pietro's wooden sticks and momentarily turned away . I had my hands full. I had to watch out for both the crab and Paulino, to keep an eye on the sharks and watch for the signs from the Professore Believe you me, I worked up a proper sweat in that cellar.

By now the crab had landed on the bed of the aquarium. Perhaps just an arm's length from Paulino. Having got there, it naturally wanted to clear off quickly and started crawling away. Paulino saw his prey and shot off after it like a bullet. He grabbed it with all eight legs at the same time and, before I could react at all, he was on his way with it back to his hiding-place. Then I pulled on the string. It came up with both of them. I'd almost reached him with the net in my other hand. Suddenly he managed to grab the tip of a rock with a tentacle and held onto it with an iron grip. Now Paulino was hanging, with the crab fixed in his tentacles, onto my string and was holding with all his might onto the rock in the shark pool. I pulled even tighter on the string. Paulino's tentacles became longer and longer. But we would not let go either of the crab or the rock. The Professore was making wild gestures and was directing me the whole time to the left and to the right. Slowly they approached. The sharks had split up and were now coming from both sides, the blue sharks from the right and the reef shark from the left. Both types love crabs and octopuses. They swam below Tomaso's and Pietro's poles and gradually came nearer from below. Paulino and my string were tightened to breaking point. He had to decide any second now whether to let go or be eaten by the sharks. Now he was twice as long as normal. Then suddenly he let go of the rock and squirted out a huge cloud of ink in which he completely disappeared. I trawled the net across the cloud, I sensed his weight and pulled him out of the water as quick as a flash. Meanwhile, the reef shark and a blue shark had almost collided in the ink cloud. They shook their heads, arched their backs and retired to the back part of the pool, deeply offended by the octopus' mean trick . I was happy to have caught Paulino with my net. Angelina grabbed him and Tomaso held out a pot that he had brought with him. Phew, that was an adventure! We brought the octopus back to his pool where the lumpfish was still waiting. Paulino didn't want to give up the crab, so we let him get on with his breakfast. We cut the string and could breathe easily for a moment. Professor Lupo later said that he had broken out into a cold sweat with fear, because he could see from the other side that the sharks would have liked to have caught the octopus but at the same time had their beady eyes on my arm. But everything turned out well in the end. However, now that Paulino was back, things became a little uncomfortable for the lumpfish once more.

Paulino and I carried out experiments together for a few more weeks. I learned a lot about his ability to change the colour and pattern of his skin. An octopus has wonderful possibilities for camouflaging itself in the sea.

At the end of my stay I travelled out into the Gulf of Naples with the two fishermen, Tomaso and Pietro.

We let Paulino slip off far out to sea, and it almost seemed as though he had given me a farewell wink with his big eyes and had waved with one of his many arms.

LEOPARD

Do you know Ceylon at all? No? That could be because the wonderful island of Ceylon, very near to the equator, has a different name nowadays to what it used to have. Today it's called Sri Lanka. In our language that means "resplendent land"

Go and ask your parents and grandparents about Ceylon. I am sure they will get all glittery-eyed and begin to have melancholy thoughts about far-away countries, the Tropics and exotic creatures and plants.

When I got the opportunity to spend some time doing research in the Yala National Park I said yes immediately. I was very curious about Ceylon, sorry, of course I mean Sri Lanka. The National Park is in the east of the island, directly by the sea and is really, really big. We wanted to find out how many leopards still lived in the National Park. Many zoologists thought that the Sri Lankan leopards were dying out. Therefore, they had to be counted. Without knowing how many there are and exactly where they live you cannot really help the creatures which live in the wild. That is true throughout the world.

One day Lisa, you remember her from the porcupine story, and I landed in Colombo. That is the capital of Sri Lanka. We left Germany on a really cold March day, there was even a little snow on the ground still and arrived in Colombo after a fifteen hour flight. We descended from the aircraft and were hit by a heat-wave. It was hotter, more humid and stickier than we'd ever imagined. It felt completely different to the dry heat of Africa where we'd experienced our adventure with the porcupine in the first story. We had to go on foot across the runway to get our baggage. That was a mess, I can tell you. Everything was lying there in one big heap. I say heap, it was more like a small mountain. Everyone on the plane took their suitcase and left. We tried to do this, too. But my suitcase was nowhere to be found. Children came up to us and asked in broken English what colour our bags were. They then ran off to try and find them. They fetched several suitcases and bags, but ours were never among them. The other passengers weren't too pleased that our little helpers ran off from under their noses with their luggage in order to show it to us. A lot of children were occupied in this way, carrying suitcases, bags and rucksacks back and forth; they could be sure that they'd get a little tip from the passengers as a reward for their "help". In the end, almost all the passengers had disappeared, our cases turned up. They were right at the bottom, in the middle of the heap and the little boys who brought them to us received their reward of course. At that time these children helped the passengers on a regular basis to earn themselves a little money .

Every time a plane landed there was a special break in the school lessons so that they could carry out their little bit of work. This system doesn't exist any longer in Colombo.

After about an hour we'd gathered our luggage together and had got our car. It was an off-road vehicle belonging to the Scientific Society who had engaged us for the research work. It was a super car, with four-wheel drive, electronic while you were on the move. On the way to our destination we wanted to pick up two other researchers who also wanted to travel with us to the National Park. We put our cases in the car and then Lisa and I set off.

Pieter is a Dutchman and had lived in Sri Lanka for some time. We set off in scorching heat to pick him up. He lived in a little village near the town of Radnapura. He had rented a very primitive hut there. There was no electricity and therefore no television, no real toilet and no running water. It was really a very primitive place. But that is often the case with us. As a biologist you don't earn enough money to be able to stay in expensive hotels. And in any case there are almost no real places to stay or hotels in the areas where the wild animals are to be found.

We had to ask the way several times to get to Pieter. That wasn't easy, because very few people that we met on the street spoke English.

Finally we arrived. Pieter was ready to go and we wanted to move on quickly, but his landlords, a very nice peasant family, offered us tea. Even though we were in a bit of a hurry, it would have been impolite to refuse the tea. So we were sat down comfortably in the hut and were telling them about our experiences with the animals when the landlords whispered to us that a dragon lived nearby and that they were very afraid of it.

"Dragons!", we said. "They don't really exist". These words did not go down very well.

"I've seen it, as clearly as I can see you", blustered the farmer and got really upset. We did not want to insult him and asked politely what the dragon looked like.

"It is much bigger than our dogs and has a golden black skin, a terribly large mouth and sharp claws. When it runs it thrashes its tail wildly. In addition on top of that?, it snarls and hunts small children."

"That sounds like a reptile", said Lisa."

"Yes, could it possibly be an iguana?", I added.

Although it was fairly late in the day, we talked the farmer into taking us to the creature. After initial hesitation he said yes. You should have seen us, as we marched there in line behind Luan, (which was the name of) the farmer. We did not have to go far. The woods got thicker and thicker and it was getting dark when Luan started to walk slower and to show signs of anxiety. He quietly crept forward until we could only push our way through the bush with the greatest of difficulty. "I hope that there are no snakes here", whispered Lisa to me. "Of course there are snakes here, but I think that they'll clear off once they hear our feet trampling feet", replied Pieter. I decided to keep a keen eye on the ground I was treading on so that I would not step on one. Luan bent down, placed his knee on the ground and made a sign with his hand. "It's back there." But we could see absolutely nothing.

"It's sitting in the branches", he said impatiently and pointed ahead.

In front of us were fallen trees whose branches were either pointed vertically upwards or were lying on top of each other. But still we could see no dragon.

We moved carefully nearer. Luan tried to hold us back. Trying to stop three biologists, like Pieter, Lisa and me is like trying to stop a speeding train - impossible. So we went nearer very carefully. What had Luan said? Bigger than a dog, black with golden spots, a long tail and a large mouth, you must be able to find such a creature.

Suddenly a head was raised and looked at us with its big eyes. It was a huge animal for a simple lizard, at least two meters long and it seemed threatening. Its forked tongue shot continuously in and out of its mouth towards us

and none of us would have been surprised if it had spat fire. But all that was nonsense! "Dragon, my foot!", said Lisa

"It's a monitor lizard."

"Monitors are also called the last dragons. So Luan was not so wrong", said Pieter who knew monitor lizards well, because he had spent some time with the huge, creepy, Komodo dragons.

We stood really still and just looked at the creature. Then, completely unexpectedly, it seemed to explode into action. It took a long jump that was incredibly fast and sprang in our direction from the thick branch it had been sitting on. We backed off, terribly shocked, fell over our own feet and then over each other like dominoes. As we were falling over we could see that the monitor lizard was still coming towards us hissing all the time and that it then moved to one side at the last minute. As it did this it almost ran over poor Luan who plunged screaming with fear into the bushes. Then the creature disappeared noisily into the undergrowth. "Now do you believe me?", he asked nervously, eyes wide open with fear.

"It was only a monitor, Luan. An animal, a lizard. It doesn't bother people normally and it was only shocked and wanted to get away", I said as calmly as I could, although my heart was still beating fast from the shock. We calmed Luan down after a while and started to make our way home.

In the meantime it was almost dark and we had a long way to go. It was a good thing that Luan knew the way. Now we had to keep an eye out for snakes. Luan advised us to tread heavily so that the snakes would hear us and disappear. That's the best way to scare off snakes. Trample about and make a lot of noise.

In the tropics, near the equator, it gets dark very quickly and we had to go through a big cocoa plantation before we could get to the hut.

In the plantation we could see the red cocoa fruit hanging above us and imagined how you could make chocolate or hot cocoa from them. We could almost smell it, because we suddenly had an incredible appetite. A little later we then reached the papaya plantation which belonged to Luan's family.

All of a sudden a booming sound rang through the air. It was as if a storm was rattling the trees and causing the fruit to fall .

"Watch out, we're too late, they're coming. My God! Now things will get really bad", shouted Luan and pressed himself with his face forward tightly against one of the trees. "Don't look up and watch out for your eyes".

We gave a start. What was going on? What was this crazy booming sound? Why should we watch out for our eyes? An instant later we understood exactly what was happening. The sky above us filled instantly with giant flying foxes. Hundreds of them sailed down onto the plantation and landed above us in the trees.

Unfortunately, these flying mammals have one unpleasant habit. Before they land on a tree they drop their pooh. It falls down and down was where we were. You know that perhaps from birds who have to relieve themselves in flight. But that's nothing compared to these flying foxes. They're incredibly huge and have a wingspan of more than a meter, and when they have to go the pooh smacks onto the ground. Like huge bats they flew above our heads and looked for a good landing place, and while they were doing this they rained the remains of the digested fruit from their last meal down on us.

"That's disgusting! They're crapping on us from all directions!", Lisa shouted angrily at the same time as a number of droppings cracked down on her. Now we understood what Luan had meant when he said that we should look out for our eyes. It was raining excrement and it would have got into our eyes if we had looked up.

Quickly we ran to thick brush or clung to a tree trunk so that we wouldn't get hit.

It was only when the many hundreds of creatures had settled in the trees that we could slip off without running into danger.

When we arrived at the hut we noticed that we were covered from head to foot in pooh. Fortunately, the creatures are only fruit-eaters, and so we had no great fear of catching a disease. We quickly took off our dirty things and washed ourselves with Pieter's water. After this adventure we said our farewells to Luan and his family and assured him that he need have no fear of the dragon and then we went to our car. The entire family waved us goodbye. We drove a little further to a little hotel where we first had a good shower. Sri Lanka's animal world had given us a warm welcome. First we had had a chance to see a rare monitor lizard and then the biggest flying foxes in the world had crapped on us from on high. If that wasn't an interesting start to our research stay, I don't know what was.

When we were sat in the hotel restaurant in the late evening we had to duck from time to time. The room had a large opening on either side to let the wind blow through, which was very pleasant in the heat. Huge bats flew through this opening and around the room at a rate of knots. They caught the insects which were attracted by the light and often came very close to us.

We three were naturally on the lookout after our previous experience, thinking that the creatures could also let a few bombs drop in the course of flight and could bring us into a regrettable state of affairs once again. And we didn't want to take a shower again before going to bed, even though we were dripping with sweat once more in the humid heat.

On the next day we wanted to pick up Gloria. Now, that was an adventure. But I'd best start from the very beginning. Do you like snakes? I mean really big, thick and possibly dangerous snakes? If you don't, then you'd better not go where Gloria spends her spare time. She loves snakes and is an expert on reptiles of all kinds.

It was planned for Gloria to be (or Gloria was supposed to be) the last person that we would pick up on our way to the National Park. She'd been taking a holiday for the last two weeks in the middle of the Sri Lankan jungle. The tiny camp in which she lived was near a river and one thing you could be sure of: there were lots of snakes there, otherwise Gloria wouldn't be there.

"It's no problem for you to wait until Gloria comes back", said the head of the camp and showed us her hut. It was full of crates containing snakes. Big ones, little ones, poisonous ones or constrictor snakes. She had caught the animals in the local area. She determined their species, then examined and marked them. Gloria had taken on two tasks: She investigated which and how many snakes were present there and additionally she caught snakes for the zoo and snake farm in Colombo. She spent her holidays in this camp and did everything voluntarily, only being paid in food and lodging. Having so many snakes around us was a bit uncomfortable even for us zoologists. If you think about the fact that Gloria slept in her hammock between all these poisonous snakes, she must have had a lot of faith in the crates and sacks in which the snakes were contained. In any case, we left the hut pretty sharpish. We asked where she had gone to and if we couldn't look for her. A little girl was prepared to show us the way. "Gloria is my friend, I know exactly where she went this morning."

No sooner said than done. We went with little Chandrika into the jungle. After a while she began to shout for Gloria. No reply. We went on. Soon we were all shouting Gloria's name. Some time or other we heard a weak voice answer and went in the direction from which it came. Then we saw Gloria. She was standing with her hair on end in a white T-shirt and shorts in a clearing. Next to her was a canvas sack and she was struggling wildly with a big snake

We ran to help her. She was holding the creature tightly with her left hand directly behind its head and the rest of the snake was wound around her right arm and her neck.

Gloria was desperately trying to get a two metre long tiger python into the sack. Sweat was pouring down her. Her face was gleaming. Whether it was joy at seeing us or because the fight with the python was so much fun was unclear at that moment. So we quickly helped her to capture the snake. Pieter held the sack open, I grabbed the end of the python's tail and Lisa its middle parts. We shoved the violently writhing snake with one big heave into the sack and tied it up. Then we brought it to the other sacks which were hanging on a branch in the shadows. Then it was time to say hello to Gloria.

The American was really a bit crazy, even as one of us animal-mad zoologists. That is how she got her nickname. Everyone called her the crazy spectacled cobra.

However, we knew nobody who could deal with snakes better than her.

After these efforts we asked her if she was prepared to travel with us to the Yala National Park.

"Sure, I've been waiting for you to come. But before we can set off I must just quickly catch a cobra. I haven't got one as yet and until now

I've only seen small ones. I found one just now. Then I had to catch the python, otherwise he'd have gone."

"And what about the cobra? Won't it have gone, too, in the meantime?", I asked.

"No, no, it's eating right now, it can't go off too far."

We carefully went behind Gloria. It was incredible how many large and small snakes she showed us on the way to the cobra. She showed us snakes where we could see none. Big creatures like the python which she had just caught, but mostly they were smaller ones or they were short and as thin as a pencil. We would have walked right past them and never have seen them if Gloria hadn't shown us them.

We came to a big tree. Its smooth yellowish bark was made up of large folds. The rear parts of a big snake were peeking out of a hole at the foot of the tree. We put the sacks to one side and Gloria told us to keep our distance.

"Stay where you are or you'll do something foolish. I can manage". She found a sturdy stick, cut it up so that it formed a V shape at the end and went over to the snake. She bent over carefully, grabbed its tail with her right hand and gave it a hefty pull. She pulled the cobra out of the hole in one jerk and threw it to one side. Now she took her stick, took exact aim and thrust it at the snake directly behind its head, pressing it onto the ground. The rear part of the snake was thrashing about wildly , but it could not rear up and bite any more. It had just eaten something pretty big. You could see that from the thick bulge behind its head.

Perhaps it was a rat? In any case it looked like the tail of one poking out of its mouth. It must be an unpleasant feeling to have just swallowed a rat which is just on its way to your stomach. The tail is still hanging from your mouth when some mean human presses the fork of a branch into your neck. Well, whatever, the rat was also not having a great time of it. Gloria called us to come with the sack. She bent over, grabbed the neck of the cobra and we helped her to place the strong creature into the sack. Done! Little Chandrika had watched us rooted to the spot with fear and we told her that she should never ever try anything like that herself. She promised us faithfully that she wouldn't. Now we went back to the camp. An hour later we had driven off in the direction of the National Park. Later on the snakes from Gloria's hut were collected and taken to Colombo.

We arrived at the National Park late in the evening. Everyone was asleep already and we were each given a little bungalow in the camp where we could sleep. There was no more dinner and so we had to go to bed with empty stomachs. We were put off with a promise of breakfast the next morning. The bungalows were spread widely across the camp so that you could hardly see your neighbour. Bushes and trees obscured the view.

There was also no electric light, only a little oil lamp. We were told that we could shower the next day in the main house. So we all sat hungry in our huts. I was tired and in a bit of a bad mood, because we had been told that we should on no account leave our house in the dark as it would be too dangerous without a torch. So there was nothing left for me but to go straight to bed. I'm not someone who gets scared easily, but I was not as familiar with the creatures in Sri Lanka as those in Africa and when I thought about all the snakes that Gloria had shown us I decided to stay put in my hut.

Sleeping, however, was not such an easy thing. Strange noises came from outside. Muffled scraping, grunting and wheezing, a pattering of hooves and then something rubbed against my hut so that it wobbled on its four corner posts like in an earthquake. I checked carefully that my door was properly closed. But when I shouted very loudly "Hey! Clear off!", the strange noise soon stopped. Then I searched every corner for snakes, scorpions and larger insects. After this I spread out the mosquito net which was hanging over the bed, tucked it in under the mattress, crept inside and carefully closed the gap. Then I lay down and quickly went to sleep after I had got used to the night cries of the flying foxes and the other nocturnal creatures.

A terrible screeching and rumbling on the palm leaf roof jerked me from my sleep. There was a bellowing and screeching as if all the spirits of hell were gathered on the roof and wanted to break in to my hut. I'd left the oil lamp burning and could see that large amounts of dust were sprinkling down from the ceiling onto the mosquito net and onto the bed. Dozens of mosquitos were lurking outside the mosquito net and yearning to get at my blood. I was glad that I had been careful in closing the net.

The row got worse and worse and all the spirits of Sri Lanka's creatures seemed to be having a fight up there. Then the sound disappeared as quickly as it had come. Silence fell and my heart started to gradually beat more easily. I swore to myself: "These stupid apes. Making such a noise in the middle of the night. Do they have to fight on the top of my bungalow of all places.

The langurs should go and disturb Gloria, she'll hopefully set her snakes on them", I grinned into the darkness and soon I was asleep once more.

The next morning came, the birds of the tropical jungle sang, twittered, screeched and howled their heads off. In the distance a water buffalo bellowed persistently. I recognized the alarm call of an axis deer and a peacock screeched directly next to my hut as if it was fighting for its life.

Peacocks can really get on your nerves, particularly when they're looking for a female. This loud, shrill Piuuuu, Piuuuu rang in my ears and seemed to go on for ever.

In the meantime I was incredibly hungry and I could have eaten a whole peacock. I brushed my ragged hair, tucked the towel under my arm and picked up my toothbrush. I wanted to run quickly to the main house to shower and have breakfast.

Breakfast, that was the magic word. Since we picked up Gloria we had had nothing to eat. That situation needed correcting immediately. I threw open the bungalow door and the bright rays of daylight streamed inside. And it wasn't the only thing that came into the bungalow.

A fat pig stormed inside like it had been bitten by a wild monkey and almost ran me over. And it was some pig. A huge light brown Sri Lankan wild boar thought that it had to chase me around in my own bungalow. And not just that. His entire family came with him. Four little light brown piglets and a pig which was totally covered in wet mud, probably the mother, rampaged around in my hut.

An instant later and the boar family had taken possession of my hut and I had no say in the matter whatsoever. The filthy pig rolled around on my raffia carpet and rubbed off the mud that was covering it. The light carpet became a complete mess immediately, as if a horde of children had stamped their muddy wellies on it. Now, you know how your mother curses !! if you do this. That was exactly what I did at this moment.

"Get out of here, the lot of you!", I screamed, but at the same time I carefully took cover behind a chest of drawers. You never know, wild boars have a fearsome bite if they are upset. My pig-visitors sniffed curiously around, stuck their snouts under the bed and knocked over both of the chairs and the table. They ran around the little hut like a bunch of startled chickens and turned over every single thing that had been standing in the room. They pulled at the curtains, got hold of my suitcase, which was closed fortunately , and dragged it around the place. Together they managed to move my bed right across the room. When they smelt something to eat in my trouser pocket, they argued amongst themselves and the boar gave the sow a powerful bite in the ear so that he could be the first one to get at my chewing gum. He immediately got hold of my trousers and, making wild grunting sounds, tried to reach the chewing gum in it. The sow also wanted to get her share and so she bit into the other trouser leg and pulled at it like mad. There was a loud RIP and my trousers were torn completely down the middle. The jeans had no chance between the teeth of those two wild Asian boars. One of the little piglets now tried to jump up onto the bed and to settle down on my pillow. The other two also made efforts to throw themselves into my bed. Now that was going too far. Before they could lay waste to the bed or tear my jeans to bits I grabbed a chair, taking it in both hands in such a way that the legs were pointing at the pigs. Then I shooed the squeaking mob to the sound of wild screaming in the direction of the door. After a short delay and some angry grunting it was too much for them, especially as they could not get at the chewing gum, and they ran off. Papa pig was the last one to leave the hut and I stood with the chair in my hand, screaming and cursing in my doorway. In front of me the whole troop of them made off at breakneck speed, grunting loudly.

And who was standing outside and laughing themselves silly? Pieter, Lisa, and Gloria. They'd been watching my battle with the pigs with incredulous faces through the open door. When they saw me waving the chair at the pigs and caught sight of my stupid expression, they almost split their sides with laughter. It must have looked pretty stupid as I stormed out of my hut screaming and set the camp pigs running. But so what? I was extremely hungry and the last thing I wanted was a bunch of pigs in my hut who would turn everything upside down and keep me from my breakfast. In such a situation I could show no mercy. The first victory of the morning was a battle with the pigs.

We got down to work the next morning. By the way, the pigs wanted to get inside my hut once more, but their surprise attack did not work this time. I shooed them off with intense waving of my arms and shouting. After that I was left in peace and the days that followed they sought out other victims for their surprise attacks. We took up our posts at places in the National Park where the rare Sri Lankan leopards had been recently sighted . We also wrote down which and how many of their typical prey we saw and of course if we saw a leopard or found its tracks. Another group of scientists looked for the few animals in the huge area which had been fitted with a radio collar and entered the details of where they were and on what day they were sighted onto a map. By the way, these were the same radio collars which we had used in Africa for the cheetahs. As I'd not seen a single leopard in the first few days my work would've been boring if it had not been for the encounters with the many other kinds of animals. And so I saw antelope, reptiles, buffalo, many incredibly colourful birds, spiders, beetles, butterflies, even one time wild elephants from a distance and of course mongooses.

I was always particularly glad when I received a visit from a mongoose family. Mongooses are quite similar to our martens and live in the savannah in large families, in caves which they have either dug themselves or have taken over from others. These lively fellows hunt insects, small lizards, scorpions and of course snakes. As small as they are, they can also be quick, brave and cheeky. Mostly they passed me by in groups of three to seven.

Mongooses, always on the move, lively and curious

They kicked up a racket and turned the whole of the area around me upside down. Every stone was turned over, every tuft of grass combed through and they poked their noses into every opening, no matter how small. Usually they found some tasty treat there, such as a beetle, millipede or a scorpion. The scorpions tried to defend themselves against the mongooses and to catch them with the sting at the end of their tail. But mongooses are quick. In fact, they are incredibly quick in shying away. I never saw a scorpion catch a mongoose despite its lightning-like speed of attack. The mongooses jumped back like a rubber ball that you throw against a wall and danced around the scorpion until they could get to him from the side so that they could bite its tail off.

That is why mongooses are welcomed around humans. They eat all the scorpions, larger insects and little insects that they can find there. As a result, the humans and their domestic animals are in less danger from these creatures than if mongooses didn't hunt there.

One day I was all alone once again on watch in the middle of the savannah of the Yala National Park. I'd set up my observation camp near to a huge rock. I exaggerate a little when I say camp. I had water, food, my camera, a walky-talky for emergencies, binoculars and a foldup camp chair. That was all. As I said, I was sat, completely alone, in the shadow of a huge tree on the lookout for a leopard which had been sighted there recently. My friends had dropped me off there shortly after daybreak and intended to pick me up in the late afternoon. It was very hot and I had difficulty in keeping my eyes open and not falling asleep.

So I was glad of the diversion that came my way. A pair of mongooses on patrol through the savannah went directly past me. I didn't move and they came nearer and nearer. It was great to see how they competed in a playful manner to take from each other the insects that they found or how they shared large beetles with their young. Even the young mongooses tried to catch scorpions. But this only caused their mother to jump up and down in a mixture of fear and anger. The large family had almost reached the tree when they noticed me and ran off screeching loudly. They ran as if a leopard was after them and I asked myself why they were so afraid of one single human. After this interruption, which had perhaps lasted twenty minutes, I looked around my immediate area.

Damn, I was a bit too late. From behind, a large herd of wild water buffalo had approached.

There were a hell of a lot of them. They were grazing and standing around the tree in a semi-circle at a distance of about ten metres and they were slowly approaching it. Wild water buffalo are very dangerous if they feel threatened. I was still hidden behind the tree, but as they came nearer I stood so near to them that I was clearly a threat to them.

Buffalo often appear in large numbers; they can't see very well and if you get too near to them, they simply attack whatever is in front of them. I was therefore in a really tricky situation. What could I do? Running off was just about the most stupid thing I could do. Perhaps I could climb up the tree. But that was easier said than done. The bare trunk was much too thick for me to pull myself up it and there was no branch within easy reach. The branches with the thick leaves began further up. I couldn't climb up onto the camp chair which was much too shaky and not high enough. The buffalo came nearer. Now I really was in a lot of danger. I could only wait and remain very still. I carefully placed the chair in front of me in such a way that it would provide any buffalo coming around the tree from the left with a small obstacle and I then clung very tightly to the tree. I remained motionless in exactly the place where the bark formed a vertical hollow. I hardly dared to breathe.

The water buffalo came nearer and nearer. I could hear their hooves stamping on the dry earth. Their puffing and their deep droning when they spoke to each other came ever nearer. Now I could smell the animals very clearly. That strong vapour which smells of a mixture of the wilderness, mud and dung which the animals carry around with them almost took my breath away. I started to sweat. I really was in a life-threatening situation . If they sensed me or took fright and attacked me, that would be the end of me. Calm, keep calm. Don't move. I couldn't show any fear. Don't rattle your teeth even if you are afraid. "That's the wild. You always wanted to experience adventures. Well, now you've got one", all these things were going through my head. Meanwhile, without me noticing them, some of the animals had gone over towards the tree. Suddenly they became restless. "Damn, now they've spotted me", I thought. I closed my eyes. I didn't want to provoke them by staring at them. This is true for many animals. So as not to rile them it is best not to look them directly in the eye. So my eyes were shut and I could hear how the water buffalo were getting more and more restless. I opened my eyes just a tiny little bit and saw that some of the buffalo were stood just a few metres away and were looking intensely in my direction. They lifted their heads to be able to see and smell better what it was by the tree.

Then, as if someone had given a signal, a huge bull took a deep breath. He reluctantly turned his head in my direction, let out a few deep tones, quickly took a few short steps towards me, stopped suddenly, threw his head up, gave a threatening roar, turned to one side and began walking away. His steps got quicker and quicker. Then others set their heavy powerful bodies in motion and gathered pace ----- away from me. They ran off into the savannah with the wild noise of their stamping hooves leaving me and the tree behind them. With the roar from a hundred throats the buffalo galloped off, turning back to look again and again. Away from me, that was the main thing, away from me. They only left behind a giant dust cloud which slowly followed in their wake and then gradually sank to the ground. Phew! My knees were shaking and my throat was dry with fear and excitement. I opened my water bottle with trembling hands and took a big swig. I also poured some of the into the palm of my hand and washed my face with it. That was a let off. I had managed to emerge unscathed once again. I had been really lucky.

My interest in carrying on my observation of the animals had disappeared for the moment in the excitement. I hoped that my friends would come to pick me up earlier than usual today. And I was lucky. It must have been four o'clock in the afternoon, the buffalo had been gone for two hours, when I heard the sound of the car engine from the distance. They came from the same direction as the buffalo had come from. I grabbed my chair and my other things and went towards them. They'd almost reached me when Gloria and Lisa jumped up from their places on the car's observation platform and pointed excitedly in my direction. They waved and shouted something that I couldn't understand, however. I waved back and approached them in a relaxed manner. Then I saw what was going on, they weren't pointing at me but at the tree under which I had been sat the whole time. I was just a few metres away when I turned round and recognized with a shock what they meant. It was sat on the lowest, thick branch and was about to jump down.

I was taken aback. It was a huge leopard. It jumped down and looked across at me, its eye sparkling as if it wanted to say, "Hey, old chap, I bet you didn't expect that, did you?" Then it turned away from me and went leisurely in the direction in which the water buffalo had gone.

I went weak at the knees. The leopard had already been sitting in the tree when my friends had dropped me off in the morning. Because I'd shown no signs of moving off it had stayed there the whole of the time.

Now suddenly I understood why the mongooses had cleared off in a panic, they'd sensed the presence of the leopard or maybe even seen it while I was calmly observing their goings-on.

Of course, the leopard in the tree above me was the reason why the buffalo had made sure that they got away as soon as they got scent of it. All that for fear of the leopard. And little me was sat comfortably directly underneath it without a clue that it was there and it only needed to simply jump down to attack me.

I was extremely lucky that the predator had no interest in bothering with me. Perhaps it was full and had slept the whole day? Perhaps it didn't really matter who was sitting down below, because it was nicer up there? Possibly it was just my lucky day. But it was particularly important, and I would never have believed it possible, that a leopard had saved me from the threat of a herd of wild buffalo simply by its sheer presence.

When we arrived back in the camp everyone found that my adventure was the craziest thing that they had ever heard, and I had to tell the story over and over again. The local Singhalese and Tamils regarded me from then on with great respect. They whispered to each other that I had a magic spell to calm leopards. Ah, if only I had. But I don't believe in this and I think that I just had an enormous slice of luck and that the leopard had a good, lazy day

We managed to survive other adventures in the Yala National Park with elephants, tigers, apes, snakes and a crocodile. But I'll tell you about that in another story.

About the Author

Dr. Uwe. H. Kullnick, Munich, is Biologist. He traveled round the world always on search of new behavioral insights in the animal kingdom. He is specialized in Zoology, Neurophysiology, Anthropology and Psychology. Beside his work for a big Telecommunications Company he did field studies in Africa, Asia, Europe and America. He writes novels, short stories, children books and medical non fiction books. As Journalist he publics columns, medical articles, glosses and comments. He is chief editor of the Journal ZEITNAH and chairman of *Freier Deutsche Autorenverband*.

Made in the USA
Lexington, KY
11 December 2016